THESE LITTLE GEMS WILL INSPIRE:

Published by Sellers Publishing, Inc.

161 John Roberts Road, South Portland, ME 04106

Visit us at www.sellerspublishing.com • E-mail: rsp@rsvp.com

Managing Editor: Mary L. Baldwin
Production Editor: Charlotte Cromwell

ISBN-13: 978-1-4162-4630-5

Printed and bound in China.

10 9 8 7 6 5 4 3 2 1

NINA'S little GEMS

WORRY LESS, LIVE MORE!

NINA AND OTHER LITTLE THINGS®
by Eloise Morandi Nash

DON'T ASK ME
WHY I RUN ...
ASK YOURSELF
WHY YOU DON'T.

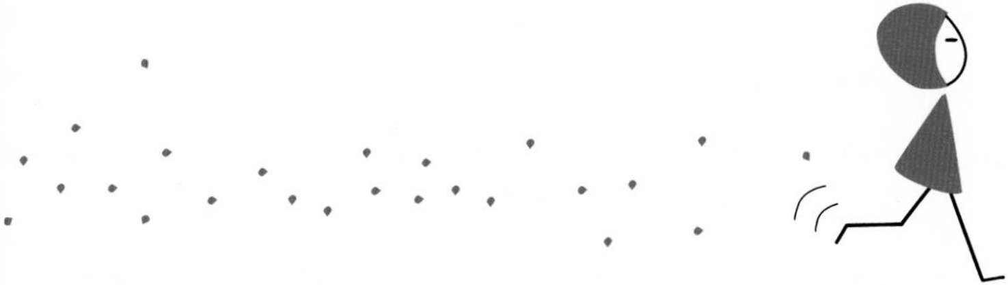

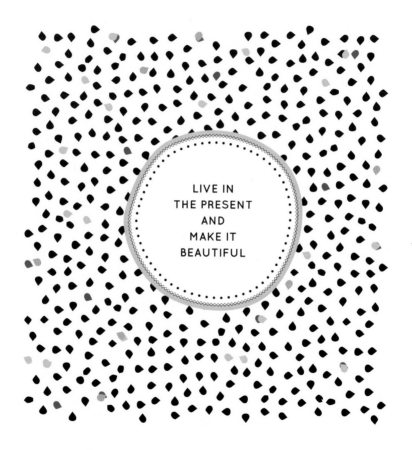

LIVE IN
THE PRESENT
AND
MAKE IT
BEAUTIFUL

~~YESTERDAY~~

NOW

~~TOMORROW~~

THE BEST
DREAMS
HAPPEN WHEN
YOU ARE
AWAKE

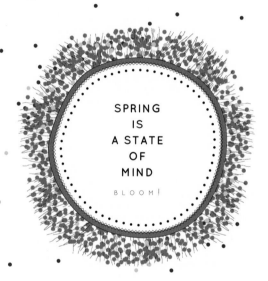

SPRING
IS
A STATE
OF
MIND

BLOOM!

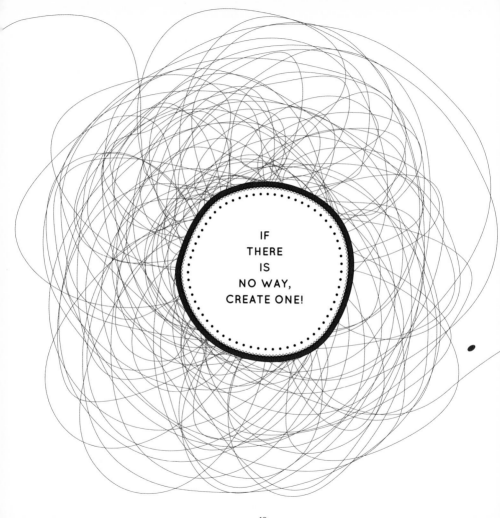

IF
THERE
IS
NO WAY,
CREATE ONE!

EVERYONE
YOU MEET
IS FIGHTING
A BATTLE YOU KNOW
NOTHING ABOUT.
BE KIND.

NEVER
MISS
THE
CHANCE
TO
DANCE!

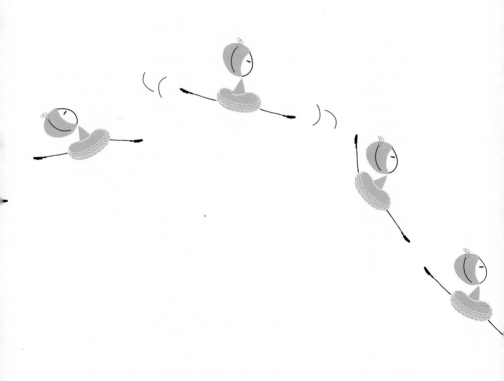

WORRYING
IS LITERALLY
BETTING
AGAINST
YOURSELF

IF
YOU
CANNOT
BE
A POET,

BE
THE
POEM.

TAPE THE SOUND
OF FRIENDS
LAUGHING TOGETHER.
SAVE IT FOR
A RAINY DAY.

LIVE
GRACEFULLY

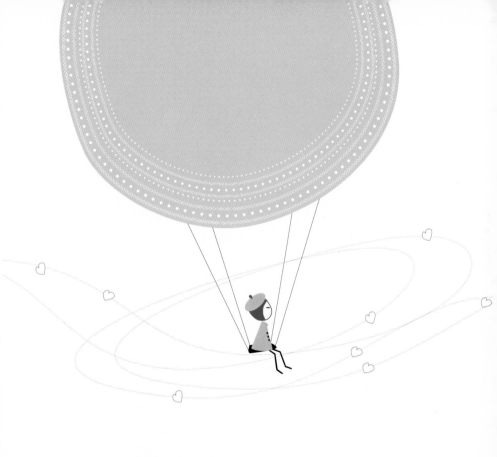

LEARN
FROM YESTERDAY,
LIVE FOR TODAY,
LOOK TO TOMORROW,
REST THIS
AFTERNOON.

THE SKY IS ALIVE
AND IT'S JUST SO
BEAUTIFUL
TO FEEL IT

FEEL THE SKY DROPS
ON YOU

DON'T BE SAD
BECAUSE SUMMER
IS OVER,
SMILE BECAUSE
IT HAPPENED

IF IT
DOESN'T OPEN,
IT'S NOT
YOUR DOOR

- OPEN A WINDOW INSTEAD
AND BREATH NEW AIR -

IF A TREE DIES,
PLANT ANOTHER
IN ITS PLACE

TRAVELING
SHOULD
BE FILLED WITH
SPECIAL
SOUVENIRS

WALK TALL,
OR BABY,
DON'T WALK
AT ALL

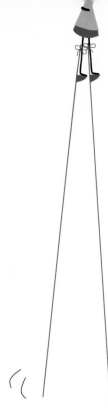

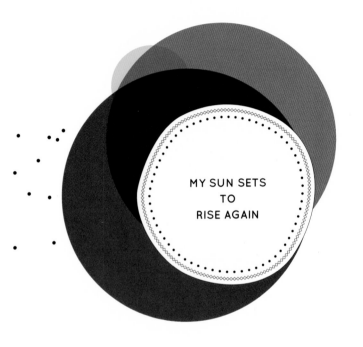

MY SUN SETS
TO
RISE AGAIN

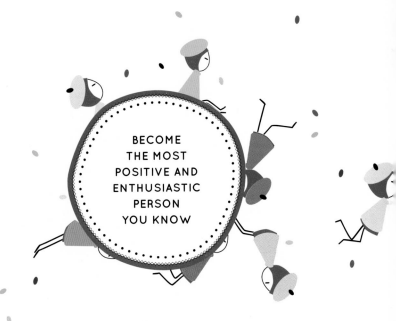

BECOME
THE MOST
POSITIVE AND
ENTHUSIASTIC
PERSON
YOU KNOW

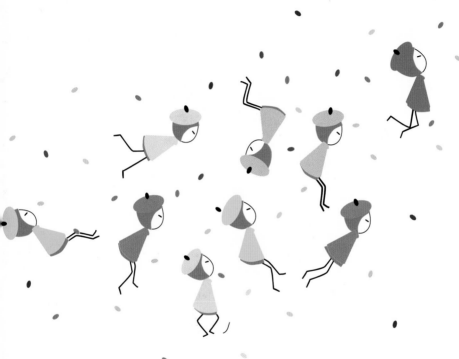

SOMETIMES
IT'S GOOD
TO HAVE
A FRESH HAPPY
TWIST!

AS MANY TIMES AS YOU NEED ONE

I ASSUME
THAT
A GLASS
IS ALWAYS
FULL

50% air

50% water

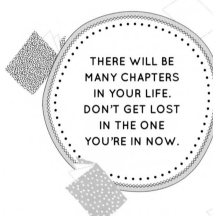

THERE WILL BE
MANY CHAPTERS
IN YOUR LIFE.
DON'T GET LOST
IN THE ONE
YOU'RE IN NOW.

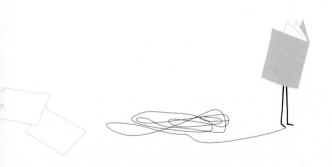

I am who I am and

I have the need to be.

Touched by all the lovely people*
who came across my life.
The ones who are in now
and the ones who will be. Eloise

*my family of coarse

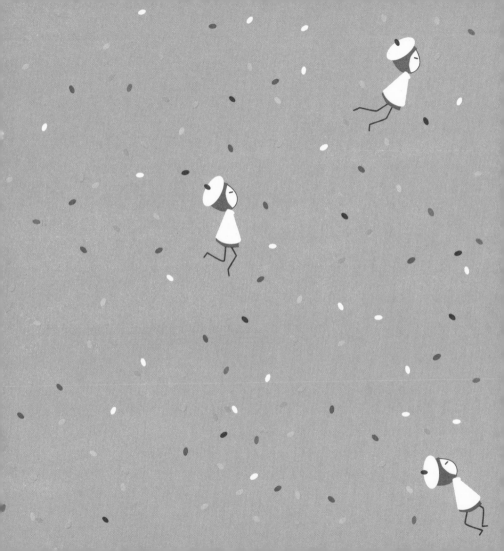

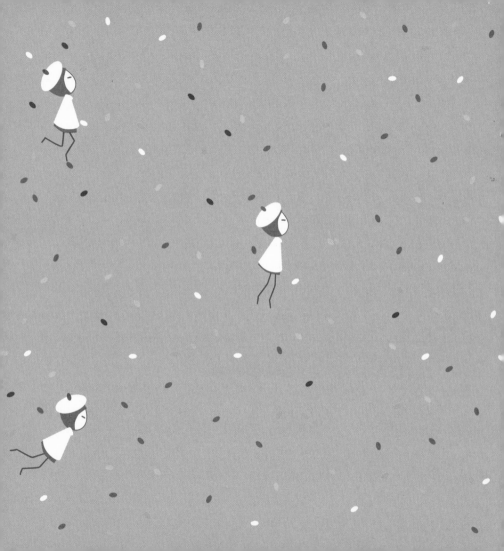